LAST LAMBS

LAST LAMBS

New & Selected Poems
of Vietnam

Second Edition

Bill Bauer

BkMk Press
University of Missouri-Kansas City

Financial assistance for this project has been provided by
the Missouri Arts Council, a state agency.

Front cover photo: "GI at Fire Support Base Wood," Vietnam
1970 © by Mark Jury, P.O. Box 194, Waverly, PA 18471
Back cover photo: "Morning Patrol Outside Da Nang, South
Vietnam" © Chuck Goldschmid, 2013
Author's photo: Kansas National Guard, 1966

"Bandolier" and "Yellow Dress" were previously published by *I-70
Review*, Lawrence, Kansas. Some poems in this collection
previously appeared in *The Eye of the Ghost* and *Promises in the
Dust* (BkMk Press).

Library of Congress Cataloging-in-Publication Data

Bauer, Bill, 1944-
   [Poems. Selections]
   Last lambs : new & selected poems of Vietnam / Bill Bauer.
-- 2nd edition.
      pages cm
   Summary: "These poems reflect how war transforms the lives
of its victims. The poems' imagery expresses how a teenage GI
in the 1960s interacts with other American and Vietnamese
soldiers and civilians and how he later confronts the war's
lasting memories"-- Provided by publisher.
   ISBN 978-1-886157-89-7 (pbk. : alk. paper) 1. Vietnam
War, 1961-1975--Poetry. I. Title.
   PS3552.A83563L3 2013
   811'.54--dc23
                                        2013039153

This book is printed on acid-free paper.

See colophon for further acknowledgments.

Born of the sun they traveled a short while
  towards the sun,
And left the vivid air singed with their honor.

    —Stephen Spender
    WWI poet,
    "I Think Continually of Those"

We are a nation of people who are afraid to speak up on
unpopular issues...

    —William J. Lederer
    in *A Nation of Sheep*
    (published in 1961)

           and what i want to know is
how do you like your blueeyed boy
Mister Death

    —e.e. cummings,
    XXI, "Buffalo Bill's defunct..."

Captain Thomas Falkenthal, a priest from the Archdiocese
of Chicago serving with the Marine Battalion Landing
Team, said he worries when he hears some troops say they
want to erase Lebanon from their memory. "That kind of
raises a caution flag," he said. "Because then it becomes a
ghost. Sometimes you have to look the ghost in the eye."

    —*New York Times*, in March 19, 1984
    article about the deaths of 200 Marines
    in the bombing of their barracks in
    Beriut, Lebanon in 1983

LAST LAMBS

AUTHOR'S NOTE

The Vietnam War officially began on November 1, 1955 and ended on April 30, 1975. I was there for most of 1969 as a soldier with the 4th of the 9th Infantry along the Cambodian Border in Tay Ninh Province and, for the last four months of my tour, wrote daily combat reports in the office of the general at the headquarters of the 25th Division.

These assignments allowed me to participate in and witness the war as a soldier in the field and as a fly on the wall in the office of a division command. I do not claim to have done anything particularly heroic. It is enough to say that I was there.

Some days I think the war only happened yesterday; other days I wonder if I was in Vietnam at all, or if I just dreamed it. Not a day goes by when I do not think of a mama-san or Vietnamese child or of the soldiers who were killed or lost body parts or plain disappeared, or of those who still serve in nightmares, flashbacks, broken lives and addiction. These tragedies occur after all wars, especially wars of no account. But the Vietnam War is my war. There is a saying that one does not have to have cancer to cure it. Yet I have met oncologists who have found themselves fighting or dying from cancer. Sadly, now they know a lot more about cancer as I now know a lot more about war.

The escalation of the Vietnam War began in 1964 with a lie known as the Gulf of Tonkin Resolution that was based on an unverified report that the destroyer USS Maddox had been fired upon at night in poor visibility by North Vietnamese torpedo gunboats. A year later Johnson himself privately remarked, "For all I know, the Navy was shooting at whales out there."

The war that followed was conducted with arrogance, incompetence, political motive and deception and ended in complete chaos and disgrace in a surrealistic event atop the U.S. Embassy in Saigon in 1975 that was televised for the whole world to see. Subsequent disclosures revealed that the 1968 Republican candidate for president, Richard Nixon, may have prolonged the war by negotiating privately with South Vietnamese leaders to wait "until after the election" to pursue further peace talks, very possibly prolonging the war to its 1975 end date. In an off record discussion in the oval office with his 1970 political group, then President Nixon stated that, "I do not intend to be the first American president to lose a war."

For most U.S. citizens the war was not much more than a television war anyway, broadcast and watched in snippets on the evening news. Estimates of Vietnamese, Cambodians and Laotians who died as a result of the war range from two to five million; 58,159 U.S. Armed Forces were killed. In 2011 it was estimated that as many as 150,000 Vietnam War veterans have committed suicide. The number of broken marriages, displaced children and cases of PTSD resulting from the war can only be inferred, but anecdotes are many.

The injustice, waste and corruption I witnessed during the war created so much fury within me that for many years I could find no words to describe what I had seen and felt and heard except for one long poem I wrote the first month back called, "Red Autumn," that I have since lost, found, and lost again. The bombing of the Marine barracks in Beirut in 1983 unleashed that fury and I wrote a series of poems that was published in a 1986 book, *The Eye of the Ghost* (BkMk Press). The book ended with "Last Poem" because I wanted the whole matter to be over and done with.

But the poems kept writing themselves and BkMk Press published *Last Lambs: New and Selected Poems of Vietnam*, which incorporated the original poems along with many others. The title of that book, which is also the title of this second edition, comes out of a line in my poem "The Last Days of the Eisenhower Administration," in which I refer to Vietnam soldiers as "...the last lambs of the nation of sheep." It derives from a 1960 book *Nation of Sheep* by the sociologist William J. Lederer. His book revealed to the general public a clandestine war that the United States was conducting in Laos beginning in 1953. In his book Lederer famously raised the issue of the passivity of the American people after World War II and their fear of challenging the government and figures of authority.

Some years later I began a short memoir, "My Welcome Home Steak," which documents the four days and nights I spent on my return from Vietnam at Oakland Army Base where I was ordered at three in the morning to eat a charred steak provided by the Chamber of Commerce as a gesture of gratitude for my service. Refusal to do so would have kept me from going home because it was a requirement on my out-processing checklist. After I told this story to a psychiatrist at VA in 2006, he leaned over his desk, shook my hand and said, "Welcome home." That was the first time I could recall anyone saying that directly to me and I wept in my arms on the worn wood of his desk shaking with the fury of all that had been stolen from me and my comrades in arms.

Here in 2013 I fear that not much has changed for the U.S. soldier coming home from a questionable conflict.

Except for World War II veterans, support and assistance for returning soldiers has been inadequate, shabby, hit-and-miss, and often staged for political show. Parades, yellow ribbons, medals, memorials and similar gestures of appreciation are fine but flag wavers have proven to be tight with their time and wallets. I can only wonder what will become of the veterans of the wars in the Gulf, Iraq and Afghanistan. They will need access to ongoing medical and psychiatric care, protection from banks, scam artists and others who feed off their vulnerability, assistance in finding meaningful jobs and holding onto their homes, families and legal rights.

I have little knowledge of what occurred in Iraq and Afghanistan other than what I have read and seen on television and what I have heard from returning veterans expressing their true feelings and opinions about how it has affected their lives and families. I tell them history has a way of settling scores. The eventual release of Lyndon Johnson's Vietnam War tapes, Robert McNamara's book, *In Retrospect*, and other exposes confirmed years later what many suspected had been hidden from the American public. The truth of how the most recent wars came to be and whether they contributed anything to the national security will one day also come under the magnifying glass of history's critical eye.

Veterans may well ask: what can a poem do to right the wrong of a war or prevent future wars? Not very much. What it can do is help to keep the record straight and give soldiers a way of expressing their anger and ambivalence without committing further violence. It can fill in the blanks, give color and imagery to the black-and-white page. A war poem can show the day-to-day life of a soldier; the sights, stench, sweat, grime and degradation of warfare, make real the fear, disgust, loneliness and true bravery of anyone with the courage to face the treachery of a bullet, mine or rocket-propelled grenade. It can tell the history of the war inside.

Once home, returning soldiers will likely face the apathy of most of the citizens they have been sworn to protect. And not long after, generational forgetting. It is said that younger generations of Cambodians have already begun the process of forgetting the atrocities of the Khmer Rouge. For many younger Americans, World War II is almost as distant as last week's email. And yet without the enormous nationwide effort to bring about a victory against the Axis powers, life today as they know it might not even exist. Three lines in a song written by John Prine, the folk troubadour poet, describe a common fate of many fallen soldiers in the aftermath of war: "We lost Davey in the Korean War./And I still don't know what for. Don't matter anymore."

I personally do not uphold pacifism as an absolute principle. The right of self-defense is inherent in human nature as a matter of survival.

I subscribe to Gandhi's statement, " Self-defense is the only honorable course where there is unreadiness for self-immolation." What I object to with the Vietnam War and other wars based on theories and speculation are conflicts initiated and prosecuted by individuals who have never been in a war and who start wars based on policy alone, personal agendas or ideology. If our leaders are to commit this country to wars like those in Vietnam, Iraq and Afghanistan, they must be damn sure that they know their history, that they have their facts straight, that they know the enemy, that our troops are well protected and that they have achievable goals. They need to be willing to listen to the advice and experience of those who have actually been in wars and stood on the battlefield. One would think that the lessons of the Vietnam War would have been lesson enough. Those leaders who want to wage war based on politics, economics or ideology need to be careful and scrupulous before they are quick to accuse others of being incompetent or weak on national defense.

I am often asked if it has been cathartic for me to write these poems. It has not. The insightful VA psychiatrist who welcomed me home advised me not to write any more Vietnam war poems, not to listen to any folk or rock and roll songs of protest or remembrance or see any movies or read any books relating to that era, not to listen again to the Lyndon Johnson tapes or go to Vietnam War memorial services for the reason that such events might only reinforce my PTSD symptoms.

That may be a fine psychological tactic but my anger is my best friend, the fellow soldier that has my back, and I will not let it go soon. I will instead keep my head down, my poems clean, well oiled and at the ready. Once a soldier, always a soldier, like it or not.

It seems that whenever there are protests or disagreements with waging unnecessary wars, the instigators turn to the flag, the Star Spangled Banner and to accusing protestors of being enemies of our country's soldiers. But soldiers in phony wars know it is not so. We know that the protest is not against us; it is for us. Many war poems written by soldiers hold up the same protest signs and sing the same protest songs, hence organizations like Vietnam Veterans Against the War. We know a little bit about fighting injustice.

No, I wrote these poems for many other reasons. For one, I am a poet by nature and writing poems from life is what I do. I wrote these poems in anger at those who perpetuated the war out of arrogance, self-promotion and greed. I wrote them as a matter of personal history, so that the boys, men and women who died or were wounded in so many horrible ways will not be forgotten to the extent that I have any say so.

As my poems strike their closing lines, they are not about me. They are about them.

* denotes a stanza break

to the ghost

THE EYE OF THE GHOST

The ghost shivers in one corner of the room
like an emigré from the moon.
You look over your shoulder
afraid it might speak.
If it speaks, you will remember.
To remember is to be a little crazy again.

The ghost remembers everything.
It has no stake in lying.
It remembers you were afraid to say no.
You stood in line with the others and cursed your luck.
The line led to the bus, the bus to the plane,
the plane to the truck, the truck to the base camp.
Rain dinged the tin roofs of hootches.
You really didn't know where you were, or why.

The ghost wanted you dead.
It was afraid, too,
digging tunnels one cupful at a time.
In the distance the floodlights of Tay Ninh
formed an enormous eye.
Bacon shriveled in the field stoves.
Ambush patrols crouched like lizards for a kill.
You spent the dry season eluding each other
and smoked when you could.

The ghost followed you home.
It was with you when you wrecked the car
and the neighbor's wife ran screaming into the yard.
An uncle told you:
"Let it go. Forget it. It's 5000 miles."
Fish in the aquarium swam oblivious to the crash
of mortars against the thin walls of daydreams.
You befriended the tree frogs and crickets again,

watched a thunderstorm blow by like twisted memory,
prayed it would carry the ghost away.

But a man meets his ghost in the hallway mirror,
brushes his teeth and locks the door.
He sleeps with a flashlight and a baseball bat.

The ghost squats in one corner of the room
waiting for the dreamer to rise and stand its post.
In its eye as it watches
from its world on the other side of the sky,
you are the ghost.

THE LAST DAYS OF THE EISENHOWER ADMINISTRATION

And that was when the young priest,
the young priest just out of the seminary,
opened the parish gym on weeknights
to keep us off the streets,
wanted us to box and wrestle
and play basketball,
cornered us one by one
demanding to know how many times
since our last confession
we spilled our holy seed,
promised us paradise if we held our fists
out of our pants long enough
to wait and sacrifice.

And when
girls like Rosemary
from the convent school
poked against us
in the wild windy midnights,
their mothers in ragged gowns
hissing through cracks
in screen doors,
girls like Rosemary
who panted until their skin shook,
then stepped back
because the good sisters implored them
not to step down,
sent us home feverish
to wait for something better,
and sacrifice.

And when
the police stalked us
through the glaring, dangerous streets

because we happened to be there,
Mexican, black, youngest in a family of ten,
and we searched alleys and trash bins
looking for booze or fistfights,
something to steal or break,
running from the young priest
who wanted us to box and wrestle
and play basketball,
tell him how many times that week
we hungered for girls like Rosemary
with their scented hair and the warm place
we could feel through their skirts,
and when the flashing red eyes of patrol cars
turned a corner suddenly,
we hid under old Chevys,
ripped our shirts and our skin
rolling over fences
to escape being slammed against paddy wagons,
to escape being beaten into better boys,
willing and ready to sacrifice.

And when
the ex-football player, the ex-marine,
the All-Christian athlete campaigning for city council,
came to our school to tell us of the vision
he had for our future and explain
how he once felt as we did, felt he knew everything,
but now he knew better, knew how we could create
a better world and be like our forefathers,
the founders of the Republic,
*

the great generals, the great frontiersmen
who believed in God, hard work and cash,
in being second to none,
and so could we
if we'd only listen and obey,
and sacrifice.

And just beyond those days
we woke one morning
in our sophomore year in college,
the last lambs of the nation of sheep,
to see the dream of our future
brighten under a banner headline
in the photograph of the rumpled carcass
of a helicopter gunship smoking human flesh
along a muddy road
in a place we never heard of, called
the Republic of South Vietnam.

THROUGH A HELICOPTER DOOR

Turn back if you haven't the stomach.
It's not like the war on television.
Oil's smeared on the air.
Rotors kick you in the teeth
with dust and rock.
The next thing you know
you're on the ground
screaming for people.
You crawl and crawl
but the only place to hide
is what you said goodbye to
when you became of age.

WAR GOD

The man in the ball cap
at Oakland Airport
slapped us on the ass
as we ran,
late for a plane,
cheered, "Go get 'em boys."
And we did.
And they did.

WILDFLOWERS

In nineteen hundred sixty five
    the planets wobbled out of orbit,

red-winged blackbirds chanted hindi
    in fields of mountain flowers and loco weed,

peace huddled under army surplus blankets
    on haiku hillsides,

big busted broad bottomed hippie girls
    with hirsute mystic armpits and moonshot eden eyes

sprouted in enchanted woods, cooing mantras,
    simmering potions, humming the wind,

danced without music, naked and spicy
    under tie-dyed peasant skirts,

hunted lost goddesses behind
    no trespassing signs on deserted farms.

A pill on their tongues,
    indian bracelets jangling,

they led us barefoot into new gardens
    on the other side of the interstate,

yes on their lips, yes to everything,
    marking the places we shared the universal Ah

with tattooed cosmic signs,
    smiling even as we stumbled away,

having no clue the glad gifts
    they sprinkled over us in acid bright midnights

would be squandered so recklessly,
    no premonition the long stemmed buds

they scattered along the unforgiving streets
    would burst into candleflame, blossom into fists.

IN COUNTRY

Fireballs blink
on Bien Hoa airstrip.
My bladder aches and I'm afraid,
but the Swedish girl says, "Stay put;
the seat belt sign is on,"
and pokes out the overhead light.
I can smell her mix
of tension and perfume,
feel the splash of woman hair
against my face
one last time.

We circle, descend, circle,
then it's morning,
then it's real.
MP's rout us
off the Northwest Orient
into a furnace
of burning shit and JP4.
"Run, run," they shout,
"Run, run. You'll miss the bus.
You'll miss the bus to Long Bien."

Mama-sans,
heads wrapped in old cloth,
lean against wooden posts and yawn.
One drags a broom
in front of the banner,
WELCOME TO IV CORPS,
and turns to look
but I look away.
I didn't know death
had such lively eyes.

MERCENARY

Gottdammit, gentlemen,
the old Nazi swore
in a nightmare accent,
master my art
before it masters you.

The garrote, he shouted,
works quiet and quick.
Make the loop on your approach,
flip it over the head,
slam your knee into Charlie's balls,
yank downward to the bone
in one eye's blink.
Sure, smartass, you can break a neck
with a choke hold, he grinned,
but you better know what you're doing.

For a night kill in a village,
he half whispered,
use a snub nose.
It's small, light, perfect
for crawling next to the target,
blasting a hollow point
directly through the ear.

Gottdammit, gentlemen, he screamed
until he must have had blood on his throat,
I want to buy you a beer some day
in a bar in Cleveland.
Make that weapon a part of your body.
Let the steel of your bayonet
lead you forward.
Don't get it stuck in the ribs, stupid!
When you thrust,
shove it up under the sternum,

shove it hard enough
so the last sound he makes
is nothing more than a sigh.

I still hear him screaming at me
to move faster—idiot!—
my grandmother'll outlive you,
taunting me in his hoarse voice
to sneak up from behind in the dark
and rob Death of another set of ears.

SATURDAY NIGHT AND POPCORN

I haven't been here long enough.
That's what's wrong with me.
I still look down
when USO girls bring popcorn
on their way to the officer's club.
I'm puzzled by the movie
lasered from the bunker
over two dozen young men
on blankets, cushions, lawn chairs,
making their beer ration last.

When the siren goes off,
I scrounge with the others
to the nearest bunker,
huddled, with no weapon.
The sound track growls down.
The projector clicks to black.
It's a war again, and even then,
someone coughs.

I wait for sappers
to toss canvas bags
into our middle: dead,
age 22, of plastic explosive.
Two MP's with megaphones
tell us the alert is over,
a chopper flipped on a power line,
pilot and gunner deep fried.

When I've been here long enough,
I'll stay with the others
to finish the movie and popcorn.
I won't go back to the hootch,
cry all night
and listen to a distant carbine
fill my dreams with lead.

MAIDENS

Water from a spigot
screwed to the belly
of a 250-pound bombshell
has the sound
of mama-sans chattering,
dunking fatigues in plastic pans.
Nothing I have said
will make them go,
and I don't care now.
I lost my privacy
at Fort Carson, Colorado.

I ignore their giggles,
try to get wet enough
to foam off
rice paddy sludge,
insect repellent,
chocolate bar,
dust on mud,
the captain saying,
"Last night's ambush was
a real success, men:
two dead,
three AK-47's,
five Chicom grenades,
knapsacks with maps."
Bodies punctured
by claymore mines.

I was there,
I wasn't there,
I don't know.
The early morning heat,
splashing water,
women's voices,

say I wasn't there,
say I'm dreaming
on a sun porch
of a frame house
in a Missouri thunderstorm.
I haven't seen my body
in six days, maybe ten.
Ivory soap sliding
off my chest
says I wasn't there.

White body, brown face,
ghostself with dirt in my nails,
image on *Time* magazine, CBS,
I bathe
in the laughter of maidens,
bomb water,
soap my hands,
my scalp,
my neck,
my legs,
my hips,
my gun almighty.
See mama, all clean,
parts still connected.
Wake me now and say
I'm already late for school.

AN ACT OF MERCY

On my afternoon off
mama-san cried
and held her jaw.
I drove her to the dental clinic
in the colonel's jeep
and read 52 pages
of Dostoevski.
Mama-san felt much better,
a gold tooth in her palm.
"Now I buy TV," she said.

MOONLIGHT AND A BREEZE

All that's left
is thunder now
and low-flying jets.
It's turning cool
and the land crabs are out.
He can smoke if he wants
and soften his grip on the stock,
but his peace will never come.
The boy who swung
on a Missouri porch
to summer wind
and an ice cream bell
lost it, lost it all
the minute he spotted a figure
in his sights,
pulled the trigger
and meant it.

THE ICEHOUSE

I. Base Camp

From where I sat
in a five-ton truck,
it seemed he'd always been there:
nineteen, no shirt,
prayer beads bangling
with ID tags,
grenade rings
around his bush hat.

They stood by the road
chanting: New guys, new guys,
greenhorn GI's.
Hey man, he said,
grabbing my gear,
move in with me.

Mostly, we filled sandbags
or unloaded trucks
or after dark on bunker guard,
sandflies biting our faces,
told half-true stories
of summer nights in Missouri.

We dreamed of a cool place,
and once on detail,
sat for five minutes
in the ice house,
a Quonset hut
between the ammo dump and motor pool.
Blocks of murky ice,
stood stacked in silver bars.

They kept the bodies there.
It was the only cool place.

Then there was an airlift
to Nui Ba Den.
You should have seen him
waiting for the Chinook,
joking around,
a stereo from Hong Kong in one hand,
a carbine in the other.
They ought to make a statue of it.

II.   Mountain

The noises at night on Nui Ba Den
are ghosts of old Buddhists they said.
Cambodian tiger one thousand years old
hides in those caves, they said.
In mists among large stones
he spliced a strobe light
into the generator,
watched it flicker
in our bunker.
Hey man, he said,
let's make it like home,
make it like Kansas City.

We built partitions with
ammo boxes, bamboo screens,
hung poster of Colorado ski slopes,

rock and roll stars.
We swung in our hammocks

to the breezes of a GE fan.
We had it made up there.

Had it made until the rocket
shredded his clothes,
blew his billfold into a bush:
photographs, laundry receipts,
prescription for eye glasses,
shot record, best part of a letter,
five dollar bill.

III. Dream

We stacked him up
naked and hard
in a dark icehouse,
his pubic hair
a blond willow tree,
his body
a silver kind of ice.

AMBUSH PATROL

To stay awake
on the jungle floor,
I analyze mosquitoes,
crawling, stinging creatures
a boy might fear,
and the confusion of why
they would laugh so loud:

my father, my brothers,
on the day the draft notice
shot up from the mailbox
as white and ordinary
as a water bill,
so eager in their bellies
for the boy famous for
his cocky mouth and easy ways
to finally pay his dues

I glanced from them
to the blossoming dogwoods
on our Missouri street,
heard the blast of claymores
I'd heard about,
felt the snap of wire
across my shins

I do not fear those here
I hope to snare and scatter,
but nights ahead back there,
three A.M., wandering a dark house,
blasting caps on my mind,
echos of the crazy laughter

of my father's sons,
the old losers at the bar
gunning for me to find out
what it's really like in the real world

SNIPER

In the mornings he went hunting,
perched in tree branches
to target a village chief

And what does he do now
this man who went hunting
for men he learned to hunt
as though they were not men
when there are no more men
like them to hunt?

And what meaning does it give
to this man now to say
as he once said to himself
sliding a round
into the polished chamber,
breathing the fume
of gun oil, cordite
and precision,
"One bullet, one kill"?

SILVER STARS

Some nights they didn't know
where they were and didn't care,
prayed the gun ships
would find an ambush patrol
caught between the Cambodian border
and the city of Tay Ninh.

When it was over and daylight came,
they got purple hearts
for their trouble, saluted
colonels and brigadiers
pinning silver
on each other's chests,
bragging how tough it was,
how brilliant they were,
hovering at a thousand feet.

THE GOLDSMITH'S DAUGHTER

"This was once a country of artisans and poets."
—U.S. Army Colonel watching detainees unload
from a truck at Cu Chi Base Camp.

Go, Buddha.
Go to the Cau Dai Temple.
Implore Jesus and Victor Hugo,
the All-Seeing Eye.
Tell them of the girl Ru,
squatting in the fishmarket.

I saw her there today,
hair hacked short,
mouth sunken and limp,
dust from the road
turning her gray in the sun.
Her family hides in the jungle.
She has sold her gold teeth,
her bracelets and chains.
They lead her through the base camps
from one bunker to another,
her nose flowing muddy like the Mekong.
Now that her lover is beheaded
she gives them boom boom
for opium and five dollar bill.

Go, Buddha.
Tell them Ru was our hootch maid.
She brought us fresh flounder once.
She swept the floorboards clean.

THE COMPANY CLERK

Let's hear it for Alphonso,
going home at last,
goddamn him anyway.

Let's hear it for Alphonso.
He had a form for everything,
the inside track.

Need a mattress or a fan?
See Alphonso.
He'll get it for twenty-five.

Got a bronze star yet?
See Alphonso.
He'll write the commendation.

Want a dozen steaks or a Red Cross girl?
See Alphonso.
He'll arrange it.

One more time for little Alphonso.
He had all the right forms.
But one.

THE BROTHERHOOD OF MAN

There was me,
the Vietnamese
and the rat.

The Vietnamese laughed
at the way I shaved,
at how I pulled my mouth
sideways and upwards
to tighten the skin.

He hung a single strand
14 inches long
from a mole on his cheek
that he stroked and admired
and held up to the lamp
so I could whistle at it.

But the warlord
of garbage and greed
mocked us both—
I shook when I saw him:
two feet high on hind legs,
strutting the spotlight
by the latrine.
He bullied the night
through a stiff moustache
and a braggart's lip,
and a shriek that sobered me
where I stood.

SHRAPNEL

A chunk of death
spins beside me
on dried mud, jagged
like an amputated arm,
like a puzzle piece
from all the days as children
we sat around a table
in a snowbound house
trying to understand
the thousand ways
sunlight fits a tree.

WARRIORS

Farm boys who could fix anything,
shoot whatever moved,
Apaches who could track Charlie anywhere,
Philippinos born in the jungle
quick with machetes and garrotes,
Puerto Ricans, headbands inked
with *Viva Puerto Rico Libre,*
forced to carry M-16s but couldn't vote "no,"
felons wanting out of jail to kill
for pay and cheap boom boom,
lifer sergeants in air-conditioned bunkers
with stolen generators for sale,
Aussies itching to hunt more gooks,
mercenaries after big bonuses,
national guardsmen holding down the draft,
clerks keeping records for generals
eager to write military history,
ghetto whites and ghetto blacks
scrawny enough to coil
through booby-trapped tunnels,
eighteen year olds marching in uneven cadence
to John Philip Sousa at Fort Polk, Louisiana
with promises of jobs they would never work,
waking years later with bombshell bellies,
blue tracers streaking toward them
into nightmare bunkers just before dawn

THE CHIEU HOI

Scrape a flounder
on a new piece of lumber.
Crack the egg on a stone
and drink it down.
War has such a sweet taste
when you're in the base camp
and the sun is shining.
For now sleep boldly
in the middle of the day
and dream your life
the way it might have been.
Give the woman a name,
any name that suits you.
Don't worry about dying until tomorrow.
Make them sweat it out.

MAIL CALL

On those days
his name is called
he hungers
for their lost voices.

Her perfumed letters ask
for money and sympathy,
the wife who demands
more than he can give.

In the dust confused afternoon
his mouth splits into what might be a smile,
not for her letters, but theirs—
his brother's fourth grade class.

Here, some become addicted to opium,
he to this monthly packet of thirty letters,
their drawings of fighter pilots,
dotted lines from muzzle flash to target.

They promise boxes of 22's,
proclaim his heroism,
send St. Christopher medals,
a plea to be careful over there, Billy.

Alone on the tarmac in a chopper's shadow,
he savors the topmost letter,
x'd and o'd with hugs and kisses,
stashes the others in his backpack.

There he holds together
with rubber bands
the only goodness
he still knows.

VIPER

The rocket left its tube,
smoked through daybreak
over the wire,
so close to Position 28
I could feel its whistle
shoot static through my ear,
hear the nuts and bolts inside
shake down to the road
and a hoarse scream,
"Somebody help us over here, goddammit."

And so it arrived.
That night
it curled itself
around the wooden skid
where I slept,
dug in so deep
I closed my eyes to it.

In the village
from a distance it watched me
stiffen at the fingers of children
pulling at my pockets—
were they children or devils?
I wondered, too,
those old women carrying baskets—
which one would strap a grenade
to the belly of a boy,
send him running at me
through the crowd?

It raced along the convoy
past ARVN soldiers
napping on the hulls of tanks

as we moved through the rubber
to Dau Tieng,
holding our M-50's two-handed,
ready for an ambush or sniper,
ready for another scream.

It breathed the rhythm
of my breath
as I lay awake
under the mosquito netting,
waiting for the rocket
with my name on it
to tear open the sandbagged roof.
I could feel B-52's shake the ground
all the way to Cambodia.
It suckered its sour lips
against my head and whispered:
Better them than you, eh GI?
Better them than you.

STUNG

Scorpions maim by instinct
Once stung, so too, those stung

Like brother scorpion,
I hide in nightmare jungles,
finger curled to ambush
men of power and gold
who order other men
to kill and maim:

I, who strike in daydreams
without remorse or fear
now that I am numb

THE GIRL NAMED "TOO TALL"

From my jeep in a convoy
grinding through the base camp gate
I watch her stoop her shoulders
to match the height of mama-sans in bamboo hats,
pucker her mouth to hide her brilliant teeth
from their beetlenut sneers.
She glares back as if I'd slapped her.
What can I do in the middle of a war
for a beautiful girl who's
six foot even, Oriental, and black?
She drops her eyes to the dusty road,
caught in a line where guards will feel her up
before she's free to scrub their clothes.

WAR DOG

I shouldn't wonder why
you give me that streetwise snarl,
all teeth and head cocked,
ready to take me on.
I'm not prepared for another fight.
You can stand me off by yourself,
a lifer like you,
back against the bunker,
a head taller now than the other hounds.

Diaz called you puppy.
But you were never a puppy
and I was never a child.
You caught the rear wheel of a jeep
and I caught this war.

I've only come back to say goodbye,
to look around and say it happened.
This has to be quick,
I'm a short-timer now,
gear's turned in and orders cut.
They don't talk to me much.
I'm one of those who'll live.

It's not my fault
I got transferred.
It's not my fault
Diaz is dead.
Not much's sure in a place like this,
not even friends.
You do what you can.
The medics stitched your viscera
into its sac.
We stayed up all night,
an hour a man,

holding your leg
so the cast would set.

I can't squeeze back
what's been torn away.
But Butterball, my little puppy,
I leave you one thing sure.
The night I rocked and you cried
we held a moment of childhood.

THE MYTHMAKER

Free falling five feet,
M-16 and grenade
outstretched as he descends
into the landmine's
fragmented soul,
he becomes mythical,
a hero to be eulogized
by those he hates.
I remember him in 1963
getting coldcocked
by a stringbean man
at the bar of the Torch Club,
victim of his problematical mouth.
Despite that and the incident
when he yanked a ballcap
down Coach Moore's porcine face,
they say he exited the chopper
screaming.

LOOKING FOR WATER

I. First Light

My boys, haggard and dazed
slept instantly in their boots
on the wooden floor of an abandoned hooch
reeking of dried urine and crusted vomit,
canteens empty, water truck late

In the universal search for water
mine was for purifying my mouth,
rank with old earth, insect repellent,
fear and spite in the early morning

Toothbrush too dry for its mission,
I knew where to steal it

My nasty little secret whispered to me:

"It's in the dusty brown five gallon cans
hidden behind the officer's tent"

The nasty little secret whispered to me:

"Steal it, corporal, in your tin cup
It belongs to you
It comes out of your ration"

Not fifty feet out,
in the seconds it takes for a nightmare
to scatter in fragments throughout later years,
the jet engine roar of the rocket
shook and rattled the tin roofs

II. Dust Cloud

I had taught my boys:

Do not light up joints on ambush patrols
Suck your thumb, play with yourself,
anything, but do not smoke or toke
Victor Charlie can smell you
Do not let him spot your match

I taught them:

Victor Charlie does not come by invitation
He will come when you nod to sleep
His rockets, her AK-47's, his RPGs,
will come whenever she, whenever he
chooses to nail your ass to the moon

I taught them from past mistakes,
mistakes a young soldier makes
because he is tired and reckless
and thinking of women:

Do not run for a bunker
when Victor Charlie sends mama-san to visit
Hit the dirt for crying out loud;
give yourself half a chance

But no, too young, too terrified to listen,
my boys bolted out of their inner darknesses,
clawed the tire marred trek of the road
for the bunker's maw,

slid right into their dying moment
as a rookie slides into home plate,
all arms and legs
in the scruff of jungle fatigues

III. Sirens

The explosion rolled me,
caked the crud and crap of war
into my eyeballs, the holes of my ears,
into the crevices of my teeth
into the thickness of my tongue

Its blast blocked my hearing,
but for the screams
of the boys of my platoon:

"Mama! Mommie! Nana! Daddy!
Karen! Angie! Pam! Jeanie!"

but for my own screams crawling
through bodies no more familiar
than road kill

"No! No! No!" I screamed,
my M-16 pointed at nothing
No! Not my boys
No, not them
No!

IV. Flashbacks

In later years an aging platoon leader
heading to his last LZ,
thinks on a park bench

He thinks to himself,
for no one else will ever get it,
will ever know

He thinks
looking for water
can be as easy as:
a fountain in a grade school hall;
a kitchen sink;

following a divining rod in a Colorado meadow;
a journey of beauty along a cascade
ending in a pool of smoothness;

a dry throat gulping cool water
drawn from under a gushing farm pump
the summer before becoming a man;

the rainstorm puddle on a sunken sidewalk
along a street of elms
a small boy dashes through;

the shallows of an ocean
where a platoon leader in his later years
can soothe his burned and spotted skull,

can find water that cannot be hidden
in five gallon cans
along coral as dead as his heart

SECOND TOUR

There was a first day
he battled the angry heat,
a stench so foul
it gagged him,
blood running down his arms
where mosquitoes struck,
a need for something cold
against his throat
so desperate
he might have killed
for ice.

There was the day
of his first firefight,
his first Tet and first kill,
his first buddy to die,
roiling stools and spongy feet,
the first time he slapped
a mama-san to the mud
with his rifle butt
and begged her to give him cause.

There was the day
his camouflaged fatigues
hung easy on his ankles,
his feet grew boots,
his helmet joined his head,
when C rations tasted fine,
the green towel around his neck
friendly as a muffler,

when he woke in the jungle morning
ready and eager.

There was the day
his orders came
to return to the World,
when he crouched by the road
waiting for the convoy to pass,
one hand around the barrel
of an M-16,
the other squeezing his dog tags,
when he turned cold
and couldn't stop shaking,
when he decided
his only choice
was to stay.

BENEDICTION

Men, the chaplain said,
my mission here today
is to pray with you
on your departure
from the combat area
and thank the Lord Almighty
you survived this tour
without death or maiming injury.
But before I get into that,
I want to remind you
there's a war going on
and it's not going to stop
because you got orders.
Even now the North Vietnamese
move into the Angel's Wing.
Your buddies are being airlifted
into a jungle
of booby traps, mines, malaria, ambush,
and you can help.
Sergeant Zigmunt has the forms.
Re-up and get a bonus.
Don't forget the early out
or assignment of your choice.
Now let us pray
in the names of the Joint Chiefs of Staff
and fixed-wing aircraft
and the napalm's orange glare
so help you God.

AGENT ASH

returning from Vietnam, 1970

The MP at Oakland Airport
pokes me awake with a sharp baton:
get it together, mister,
straighten your tie, put your shoes on,
sit up, act military,
you're not civilian yet.

I want to kill him,
such an easy thought now.
I look for a 45 or Bowie knife,
consider a kick to the head
sending his eyeballs back
to where they came from.

I know something's wrong;
I can feel it.
It's the smell of the village
after the napalm,
digging for bodies
curled crisp.

What's wrong is
the rocket that shook
Tay Ninh Base Camp
disconnected my heart
from the rest of me
and covered it with ash.

After my plane lands
I'll step onto a freeway
in the plume of a Greyhound bus,
bony ass and shaven head,
so turned around I won't remember
what I was like back then.

Cars will skid to avoid me
dragging my duffle bag
over the median,
people will gawk
at the jungle rat
marching to an odd rhythm
with a left, a left,
drop and fire.

PRIVATE ARMISTICE

Phillip, my little brother:
in the photograph
of my homecoming
I see hands hold you high
over friends and uncles
and you don't know me:
one hundred twenty-seven pounds
in dress greens,
the sides of my head
still shaved white,
my new smile
a covert operation.

RABBIT HUNTING

I

Slugs from a twenty-two pump
shattered the snow.
The rabbit zigzagged grass clumps
frozen stiff above the surface,
tumbled high in the air,
recovered, bounded into the woods.
They chased it five minutes or more
before losing it in the twisted
scrub oak, gullies and piss elm.
Uncle Joe was there, Little Joe, Robert and him.

The woods held the cold close to the ground,
numbing his feet in his boots.
He had not fired the shotgun that day;
they cursed a wasted shot.
He kept thinking of beef stew and hot chocolate,
heat by the stove in the farmhouse.

Then he saw it bobbing in the brush,
circling away from their voices.
It clawed forward, dragging its rump,
leaving the snow red.
He waited until it reached the ditch
not five feet away,
watched it paw down the slope,
flattened its head with a direct blast.

II

Home two weeks
he buttoned borrowed corduroy,
walked in a line

with his cousins and uncles
as they always had,
heading north from the tractor shed.

Not twenty yards out
a rabbit behind a combine wheel,
a small gray rabbit,
panicked, paddled a drift
for a place in the trash pile.

He squatted, sighted, military style,
elbows on his knees, ready to fire,
but stood up with a blood oath:
I will not shoot another living thing.
By God, I will not.

THE RECRUIT

The girl of warm hands will never
understand why he has forgotten
the tick tack of the rain
on the shutters of the old house

She walks beside him
on the first day home
in the silence
of an unseen rain

Said he only wants to listen
to the soft brush
of leaves overhead,
be fifteen again

TAPS

My Uncle Roy
drives a truck
that spreads salt
during snowstorms.
He doesn't want to hear
my yakety-yak
about Cambodia and all that.
The world's already got
too much shitass misery.

WAR STORIES

Old men of the VFW—
put down your mugs
and listen up.
I have a story, too.
It's about the face
of a second lieutenant
I keep seeing in my dreams.
He staggers bareheaded
onto the road,
the road out there
in the rubber plantation.
He's holding up
a No. 10 envelope
with the remains of one of your sons,
bone slivers
scraped with a bayonet
from the hull of the APC
he sent down Highway One.

He just keeps coming at me,
holding out someone's soul
for the U.S. Mail,
his face a map
of all the roads we marched down,
one boot after the other
into all the trophy cases
of your goddamned VFW halls.

You tell me how it ends.
You got all the answers.

SIDE GLANCE

I am the bastard boy
of the World Wars,
born into a violent time
in a violent country.
Violence is what I know.
Violent is what I am.
But don't worry, mister,
I won't kill you.
My dreams more than satisfy this urge
to lick the bones of the dead.

FRAGMENT OF A LETTER

Tommy, all the short timers say
they'll write when they get home.
They never do, they
disappear into a future
we'll never see
with a girl we'll never know.
The face of the girl
who keeps coming to us
in dreams
fades quickly in morning confusion,
makes us sick with envy
wondering who she's loving now.

I won't be like the others, Tommy,
I won't forget to write.
I'm going to write you
every time I'm back over there,
on days I can't think straight,
days like today in this autumn light
so red and so orange
I think the trees are crying.

In this red autumn
they're burning fires
making the air hazy and distant
like a day on the rubber plantation.
The smoke burns fresh,
the aroma of a newly lit cigarette
in a wet pine grove.

When I start laughing to myself
no one sees what's so funny.
They don't know it's you I'm laughing about,
you who could always make me laugh.
You could hardly move your mouth,

and you said, "Now look at my fucking face.
Now I'll never have a girlfriend."
None of us could stop laughing,
not even the medics lifting you
into the chopper as fast as they could.

Back here everybody's laughing
in a different kind of world.
I don't know what to say,
who to tell it to
or how to make sense.
I move with the crowds,
don't recognize any faces,
don't know the words to their songs.

I watch the news,
waiting for you to reappear
in backpack and fatigues,
waiting to hear you speak again.
And I don't know where you are
or how to mail a letter
to a dream of a war
I was in a long time ago.
That's all you are, Tommy,
a dream, just another beatup
dragged down fucked up dream
I had one humid year
when I was too young to know better.

Don't get the idea
I forgot to write,
because I will finish this letter
one day soon
and put it in the mail.

SWEET TINNITUS

My M-50 gave me arms and legs,
flanked my liver and spleen,
kept drool off my chin,
fought off catheter and bed pan,
blew away crutches and wheelchair,
pumped itself round by round
into my nightmares,
and its report rings in my ears
all day long
to remind me I'm still alive.

JOY

The soldier who kills for fun can laugh at
anything, but the man who was robbed of his laughter
by the killing searches for it everywhere. Sometimes
he encounters the shipping crate in his basement and
says, "I should have thrown this away long ago," and
pries open the lid. He sorts through the socks,
underwear, camouflaged boots, medallions, propaganda
leaflets and a pearl handled Bowie knife inscribed with
his name and "4th of the 9th Infantry, Manchu." "I
should have thrown this away long ago," he says again,
trying to feel how it was, the day after first grade,
slamming the metal wheels of his skates to the sidewalk,
the wind lifting him up by the hair, and laughing,
laughing, laughing. But his voice only circles the
barrel of his throat, his laughter mute as army green,
coarse as a kettledrum.

THE LIVES OF SPIDERS

Home from a war of long ago,
alone with shadows,
I roam the house on all fours,
face up at the ceiling,
until I find the dark
under the pool table

The carpet feels safe and soft there

Distant cousins of chaos,
they creep along side me
in six cautious steps
seeking peace
in the knowledge of shadows

MOUNTAIN MEN

I see them hobbling
    down foothills
where I live now in retreat,
    what's left bulky on their backs,
obscure as porcupines
    under folds of stocking hats
and runaway beards,
    buddies, brothers,
uncles, fathers, cousins,
    circling a lost LZ.

I see them puzzled at highway exits
    like elk or bear
when winter lasts too long,
    a species still wanting to live,
destinations scribbled on cardboard signs,
    ears tied with bandanas
hiding the sound of the torn air
    that split them through the middle,
the sound no one can explain,
    that no one else will ever hear.

WHAT THE WAR WAS ABOUT

Some said rubber plantations,
some oil,

some said gold,
some dominoes,

some said land reform,
some Reds,

some said rice,
some contraband,

some said John,
some Lyndon,

some said napalm,
some lice,

some said herpes,
some pot,

some said hippies,
some pigs.

Nobody asked us.

OLD MEN

There is an old man
who has done his work,
plowed up and down freeways
or the circumference of a cornfield
until the dull light nearly blinded him,
who has heard again the mortar round
and slumped over a steering wheel
on his way to dinner
on his way home from a war.

That old man
wishes a boy well, squeezes
his shoulder, sets aside tomatoes
on the countertop,
hands him a vintage rifle
to hang above the fireplace,
teaches him war is no boy's game
and to be with a woman wisely
he must weather well on the cold days.

Another old man resents
the swelling of his knuckles,
curses the Dianas jogging past
as he half steps the boulevard.
In his late night wine
he sees the shaving of a soldier's head
and rows of bunks in barracks,
wishes the boy no better that he had
and prays for worse.

That old man
demands the end of rock and roll,
mourns the rotting of his uniform,
the signing of the truce,
dreams boys into the Balkans,

blackens skylines with waste.
Banners in the square only stiffen his leer.
His tanks will chew the bodies of the young
even as they chant at his bronze feet.

THE WAR EFFORT

In 1942 jhowardmiller, illustrator,
found Geraldine Doyle
on a B-2 bomber assembly line,
put her on a propaganda poster
for the War Production Board
that read, "We can do it!,"
scarf knotted behind her head,
sleeves rolled up manly arms,
eyes hard with a killer's wish,
and she became known in history
as "Rosie the Riveter."

In 1970 during the Vietnam War
I stood next to a young woman
known in protest marches
as Sister Morningstar,
a flower girl in angel white robe,
peace lilies in her hair,
pumping high a cardboard sign,
shouting "We can do what?
WHAT?"

LARRY'S LAMENT

Sylvia knew Larry knew,
and Larry knew she knew
she was lying,
knew about the difference
no left leg would mean,
knew that metal thing
they called a leg
wasn't a leg nearly like
his blown off leg,
and Larry knew after Thanksgiving Dinner
at his parent's house, her smile off center,
she knew she wouldn't be
coming around very often
in the holiday dress
he bought her before he left,
wouldn't be coming around
no time except
every other minute
in his mind

GOLDEN REVOLVER

You finally jerk the barrel
from the night imp's sausage grip,
only to discover the slick alloys
sweat kidney warm in your palm.
You hate him for taunting you with it,
the wand you never dreamed you'd flourish,
but he slips the handle smoothly,
into the fingers of your fear.
You hate him for knowing you so well,
the daylight pacifist ready now for sleep,
holstering an American dream.

WORST IN MEMORY

Oldtimers claim it was
the worst in memory, snow
high as houses, blocks of ice
smashing off roofs, accidents
on the freeway, screams and broken glass.
Some went up the mountain and were lost,
buried forever in drowsy white.

I dreamed of masks, the worst of the century,
the most casualties, massive injuries,
war impersonal. I watched them milling
in airports for the first flight out:
Stalin, Hitler, Tojo, Mao, Khomeini,
Sukarno, Franco, McNamara, Saddam,
Pol Pot, Karadzic, Syngman Rhee.

I had nightmares of you leaving.
So many phantoms rise when the air
grows dank. I tried to
rouse you, explain it was a season
screaming through our evenings that numbed us
so we could no longer speak
of anything but gray.

Now it's over. My mouth reeks of bombwater,
my tongue of gun barrels. I stare through
the window for radiance and poppies. The clouds
break but snow still sits outside the cavern
of our great doubt. We struggle to wake
and forget; we raise out teeth for sugar.
The anima claws outward for bright.
That is the promise.

THE MEDIC

It's over now, John,
you didn't make the history books.
You've got to go back,
pay off your mortgage.
You can't smoke pot anymore
to get yourself out of bed.
Your kids will want more
than slogans and rock songs.
You'll have to do more
than slouch on a front porch
and stare into sunsets.
Nobody'll care about your
blood and gut stories.
No one will believe what you saw,
what you did, what they did or what
the Department of Defense is hiding.
Your letters will go unread.
You'll grow bitter and mean
like old men at Veterans Day parades.
The G.I. Bill won't pay for your anger.
Crazy doesn't count.

ASSASSIN

They shouldn't have done that,
tear him out of graduate school
as recklessly as people rip a page
from a public telephone book

They set his brain on automatic:
here is how you place the barrel of a 38
behind the ear of a village chief while he sleeps,
here is how to come from behind with a garrote

Lyndon Johnson died peacefully during a nap
McNamara wrote a book
The assassin was discharged
into the rest of his life

ONCE A SOLDIER

That instant along the Cambodian border
when the tip of his right index finger curled
into the comfortable curve of metal,
he touched for the first time in his life
the slick, sleazy subject of evil

At eighteen, ordained a soldier,
a soldier at eighty,
forever to act on impulse,
think sharpshooter, point man,
platoon leader, survival

From the first salute, an unseen soldier,
shaven head and sinister grim,
stalks within, stalks relentlessly
in malls, on busy streets, hiking trails,
always ready, always there

Eyes fixed in the back of his head,
trained to obliterate,
he knows he can take out
any man who dares him

Hand wired, ready to explode,
once a soldier, always a soldier,
condemned to wear the uniform,
endure cold, desert dry, hunger, gore,
he still serves

The war is over, he alone knows
why he marches automatic,
cries when children sing,
snaps cold without warning

"Yessir!" is what he's drilled to shout
"Yessir!" echoes in his daydreams
"Yessir! is the man he has become

MISSING IN ACTION

The young corporal
wants his arms back,
and his girlfriend,
and two hands
to cut up Thanksgiving dinner
before it gets cold

He wants to play again
in the Turkey Bowl
at his boyhood park
with high school buddies
like he used to
but they went missing
into first homes
with wives and kids
playing in the backyard

He wants what else he lost
on ambush patrol outside Tay Ninh City
and to hell with a Bronze Star Medal
and a disability check and
a "Thank you for your service
to your country"

A VIETNAM VETERAN'S MEMORIAL DAY

We weep today for those
whose names are carved on this wall,
for those whose bodies
tumble in distant waters,
for those who've never returned
from the dust of another country.

We weep too for these old soldiers
standing here to the boom of the guns
and the haunted brass of bitter bugles.
They empty their tears for themselves,
for the lies they believed,
for the boys they once were
before they learned to kill.

WARNING

for vandals of the Kansas City Vietnam War Memorial

Don't mock this wall.
Don't say these soldiers
didn't fight a real war.
While you watched playoff games,
they crouched in the mud
and missed their women.
They are the sixty thousand,
robbed of their youth
by men in press conferences.

Don't mock this wall.
Don't say these soldiers
wanted to make war.
They only wanted to live out their dreams.
They just wanted to be like you.
Slide your fingers over their names
and tell me you can't hear
the echo of their voices
chanting *peace, peace*.

Let this wall be.
It belongs to them.
They paid for it.

A PLACE IN HISTORY

Guardians of the Free World
wanted a place in history
so they sent us into rice paddies,
canteens half full of warm water,
heads full of lies.
Some who made it back brought
lice, rotting feet, herpes,
a hunger for highs, half a soul.
When our time came
to find a place in history,
they hid that chapter in archives
so no one would know.
Now that the guard has changed
we stand in their place
with what we were given,
giving them back the scourges
they bequeathed in arrogance,
preserving in nightmares
their grim estate.

BANDOLIER

I thought I'd turned it in
once and for all
at Long Bien

And yet I sling it across my chest
heavy with grenades,
loaded magazines;

tell my young son,
"The war is over"
I fight it;

promised my baby girl
I'll take it off
but can't;

lie to my lover
I left it there and
she smiles

One day I'll toss it
into a rice paddy
of never been

Until then I'll bear its weight
and drag it into flashback afternoons
with no sense of honor

I never fought for my country,
only for Tony, a black guy from Detroit,
who humped with me into Cambodia

THE RETURN

Forty years gone, Sam, so many rains ago
the hulks of abandoned choppers turn red in the heat,
and I have come to take your spirit back with me

Young Vietnamese smile and gawk at my gray hair,
swarm into Uncle Ho's city on motorbikes
through puddles of stench
for their ration of socialist hope

The Hotel Rex, where the war was lost,
gleams cool in marble and granite
At guest information,
the communist seated at the desk,
her hair twisted into tight bun,
asks what I did in the war,
and faintly gloats

Out of spite, I want to remind her
of the final score,
three million to fifty-eight thousand,
but hold my fire:

I've seen the graveyards of Viet Cong martyrs,
the heroines of the Women's Union
waving red flags with yellow stars

Gondolas lift American tourists up Nui Ba Den
where you lost your face to an RPG

Before we can crawl the tourist tunnels at Cu Chi,
Charlie orders us to watch a fuzzy film
of a VC mowing down Marines with an AK-47;
78 dead, he beams, in less than forty minutes

In stalls along the road,
the inevitable dog and monkey
nip at each other, still at odds,
their masters leering at us from plastic chairs
but loving our money

Nothing left here to fear or mourn:
Time, finally, Sam,
for us to come home

AFTER THE ACCIDENTAL BOMBING
AT BAC MAI HOSPITAL, HANOI

The Communist professor of cardiology,
jolly and welcoming as he is,
becomes philosopher as he thinks back,
believing to this day there's much virtue
in being short

After the ringing in his ears subsided,
in the silence and numbness
that follows flash and explosion,
sprawled on the floor
he smelled cement
and the breath of the bomb

He felt his hair, his forehead,
nose and jaw: all there
Where then had it come from,
the hair, blood and brain matter,
splattered, sticking to his white coat?

At that moment, no one had yet
cried out, moaned or sobbed
His legs felt too heavy to move,
the vault to memory locked shut

For an indeterminate amount of time
he pulled at its latch, pulled at it, pulled at it,
puzzled its combination until suddenly,
it sprung open of its own accord

Ah yes, that was it, the conversation they were having,
the short Dr. Kai and the tall Dr. Nguyen,
his head perfectly framed in the open window

— *As told by Dr. Kai, Hanoi, 2000*

ORDER OF BATTLE

Memo To:

The President and Secretary of Defense;
senators and congressmen
who vote for war but never in one;
generals and colonels who seldom
face an enemy soldier eye to eye;
men and women over 18
who've never been in combat;
mothers and wives proud
to send their sons and lovers
to die in another country:

You want a war,
you take point

WASHINGTON, DC

Until they see
a 19-year-old soldier
with no face
before he's zipped
into a crumpled bag,
podium warriors won't know
one thing, not one damn thing,
of a folded flag
or a body on the ground

WERE THEY THERE WHEN....

Oh, sometimes, it causes me to tremble, tremble, tremble
   —"Were You There," African American spiritual

....their sons and daughters lost
their arms and legs and faces,
their youth and joy and lives
at Ka-san, Ia Drang, Fallujah, Kandahar,
those flag wavers who know all about
battlefields and heroism,
second stringers who served but never
threw in for ambush patrol,
those never in combat who love
to tell war stories and march in parades,
the shysters of Fourth of July and Memorial Day sales,
politicians of sad excuses and devious deferments,
kings, aristocrats and generals
who rally their troops from behind the lines,
promise booty, glory and a gravestone
at Arlington Cemetery

Were they there when all hell broke loose,
the recliner brigadiers of the television wars
or did they sit back, prop up their feet,
raise their glasses in air-conditioned homes,
watch neat little bombs on virtual screens
penetrate windows and bunkers
with pinpoint accuracy
thousands of miles away

Were they on foreign soil
when they cheered the children
of the Revolutionary War
to fight false fights to save the sorry ass
of the greatest country in the whole world?

Sometimes they cause an old soldier
to rage, rage, rage....

YELLOW DRESS

Last off the plane
just home from the war
from my window I saw you
leaning against the railing
at the bottom of the ramp,
a single lily in your hand,
wiping your eyes
with the hem of your dress

Odd to hug you,
to tread barefoot on foreign carpet
that first afternoon
in the apartment you rented,
still too dazed to foresee
that the drooping flower,
those tears for yourself
would color all our seasons
yellow

I had such great plans for us
the last day I loved you

FACELESS MAN

"Fundamentally the marksman aims at himself"
—Zen in the Art of Archery

Home from the war
the only way to sleep was
to fire tracer rounds into
the figure of a faceless man

When I could no longer stomach
shattering the body of a faceless man,
the 60 caliber rounds became arrows
piercing his forehead

When I could no longer face an arrow
splitting the skull of a faceless man,
I startled an elk in night vision with a crossbow,
shook as it leapt and dropped

When I could no longer let go an airborne shaft
into the solid neck of an elegant elk,
I elevated my arrows into the limitless universe
and saw at last the face of the faceless man.

LAST POEM

Today I wrote my last Vietnam poem,
fifteen years after the fact.
Those folk songs, those anti-war chants—
I couldn't get rid of them.
I'd hear someone screaming,
shattered or shot;
I'd plan my revenge
for gung-ho colonels and academic fools.

But alone in a house
in the middle of February,
I only see a familiar room.
I can look out a window
into a brown and leafless wood
and know there's an end
to anger and sorrow.
I guess you just retire it.

I've told them
all I know.
You can rest now.

ABOUT THE AUTHOR

Bill Bauer, a native of Kansas City, Missouri, now lives and writes in Hawai`i. Prior to the sale of his company in 1992, he was a co-founder and the president of Media/Professional Insurance, Inc., a firm specializing in defending the First Amendment rights of the media.

His National Guard Unit was activated during the race riots of 1968, and he was sent to Vietnam the following year.

Eye of the Ghost, his first published work, won the 1985 BkMk Press Missouri Poet's Award. He is also the author of *Promises in the Dust* and *Pear Season and the Boy Who Ate Dandelions.*

He graduated with a degree in English Literature from Rockhurst College in 1965 and worked as a reporter for the *Kansas City Star.* He is married and the father of two children.

INTERVIEW WITH BILL BAUER

by Susan L. Schurman & Linda D. Brennaman
March 2013

Q: How did Last Lambs *get its title?*

A: The United States engaged in a secret war in Laos beginning in 1953. It arose out of a concern about the perceived growing communist threat in the region. It was another case of the peasant population fighting for their rights against a repressive regime and colonial control. The guerilla war was fought by the Pathet Lao who identified themselves as a socialist/communist group and had some backing from the Soviet Union. The sociologist, William Lederer, wrote a short book, a white paper, in 1961, *A Nation Of Sheep*, exposing the war and in the process he criticized the American public for being passive, averse to questioning authority, which he speculated leads to government secrecy and endangers democracy.

The sixties signaled an end to the conventionality and denial after WWII that has led ultimately to the crisis we have today in the economy and society. Therefore, I see the Vietnam soldiers, draftees and volunteers alike, as sacrificial lambs, the last lambs of a government controlled by wealth, an established Old Boy's Club and authoritarian political power.

My take on titles.

Q: The tone of Last Lambs *seems almost reserved, considering the intensity of the subject matter. Did you intend to show restraint in these poems, or is there another explanation for this tone?*

A: This is a good question. By coincidence, I recently attended a reading at the Maui Arts Center by W. S. Merwin who lives in a small place upcountry on Maui called Hai'ku. (I think his choice of that location had more to do with the cost of the former pineapple plantation that he bought thirty-some years ago rather than its serendipitous name). Though he is known as a Vietnam War critic, I have not read any war poems he has written, though I am sure there are some.

He read one poem about an elephant who had gone mad, pulled away from its chain and gone on a rampage. He prefaced the poem about the danger of allowing anger to destroy the possibilities of imagination in art and literature. His point was that anger, while it was a powerful force in art, could be destructive to the imagination if it was not restrained, that it could easily lead to bombast, demagoguery, hyperbole, preaching, speech making, etc.

That's a long way of getting around to answering the question. I do not like definitions of poetry; I find them meaningless, but that doesn't mean I haven't learned something from them. With respect to Wordsworth's phrase, "contemplated in tranquility," I agree with the idea that whether a poem leads to metaphor, narrative, factual imagery or other means a poem calls for to strike the nail on the head, the poem generally speaks for itself using the content of the idea, place, situation, person from which it derives. True, a poem can't just be a litany of images or similes; it does need an attitude. But before a war poem explodes, it needs to have a shell, powder, shrapnel, so that when it is launched an explosion occurs.

Q: In the poem "Taps" you mention that Uncle Roy doesn't want to hear about your war experience. Have you found this a common response to your attempts to tell your stories to other war veterans as well as civilians? How has this affected you?

A: When I returned, I found no one wanted to hear about what I had learned or experienced in the war. To them, even my close friends, I seemed an oddity. It wasn't that they were critical of me; they knew I had been drafted and opposed the war. It was just that I was different. I didn't fit in any more. I had changed. They had nothing in common with me nor I with them. They had married, bought first and second

109

homes, had small children, good jobs or started their own businesses, and I had nothing except a wife who had become psychotic in my absence, which alienated them even more. My family of ten children had never been close. The war had gone on for a long time and everyone seemed bored with it and wanted to move on.

The veterans I knew never wanted to see each other again. We were tired of the war, too. We didn't want to think about it. We didn't want it to take up any more of our time and energy. We had no outprocessing, no follow up, and for many years, no real benefits except for the G.I. Bill and medical assistance for those with severe physical injuries or who were psychotic.

My mythical Uncle Roy who worked for the state highway department had been wounded in World War II and thought of the Vietnam War as though it was a threat to national security and the protestors were simply cowards and druggies. He thought they should be drafted and sent to Vietnam as a way to teach them what the real world was like.

My ex-father-in-law who was basically a good man, a Marine wounded three times on Iwo Jima, suffered from PTSD, but was in denial and became enraged anytime I tried to tell to tell him what a mucked up situation Vietnam was and that I had seen almost immediately that we were fighting for the wrong side. He wouldn't hear of it and I often got the "love-it-or-leave-it" line. After a few incidents of that kind, I kept it to myself. As for my friends, they could not seem to comprehend what I told them so, rather than alienate them further, or frighten my emotionally fragile wife, I just learned to shut up about it.

Q: The poem "Wildflowers" seems to address the changing public sentiment about the Vietnam War over the years. How did you experience your return to the States from that war. How does that affect you to this day?

A: If anything was lost in the assassination of John Kennedy, the war contributed to that loss of hope for a different kind of society in America, a society based on love rather hate, cooperation rather than competition, human values versus economic values, acceptance rather than rejection, openness rather than locked gates. Two things contributed to the disintegration of the hippie community—the war, and drugs. Vets returning from the war added to the burgeoning drug culture, brought back herpes and other venereal diseases, families broke apart, marriages failed, young people became cynical and discouraged by lies, fraud, and utter materialism. Other Americans feared the new freedoms; they reacted against it with police violence and legal retribution. Many dropped out. Many talents were lost. No one was listening.

Q: *The title of the poem "Benediction" seems to be ironic, in light of the poem's point of view. Did you, as a soldier feel let down by how the military dealt with spiritual concerns?*

A: The chaplains I encountered were of two kinds: those who were really religious beings and those who were soldiers with collars. They were logically torn by their duty to the military and their duty as so-called men of God. There was really nothing they could say or do to provide honest answers to moral questions whose answers were obvious but could not be advocated because they would be contrary to the military mission. Most of the soldiers I knew didn't have a strong religious belief; few attended services unless they were forced to. I went to confession once just so I could talk in private to someone. The man listened and was nice when I told him what I thought about the war, that I thought it was wrong, that we were fighting for rich people against poor people, slaughtering women and children with horrible weapons like napalm and scatter bombs, land mines and 50 millimeter machine guns. The only morality I found agreement about where I served was that we wanted to work together so that we could go home. The song we sang most often was not "That Old Rugged Cross," but "We Gotta Get Out of This Place" by The Animals.

As for irony, I hope it can be heard in some way through

most of the poems. It is one of the aspects of literature and art I most enjoy.

Of course, I think it must come naturally. True irony exists in nature. All we can do is try to catch it.

QUESTIONS FOR DISCUSSION

1. The poet explains why he chose the title *Last Lambs*. After reading the poems, what meanings do you find in the title?

2. Bauer dedicates the book "to the ghost." Do you think that the ghost's identity is revealed on the last line of the first poem, "The Eye of the Ghost"? Do feel the presence of this ghost elsewhere the collection?

3. Which, if any, of these poems could have been written by someone who had never experienced war firsthand? Does poetry require first-hand experience?

4. What images form in your mind as you read the poem "Wildflowers?" How do these images intersect with any other thoughts you carry about the years the United States was at war in Vietnam?

5. The term benediction ordinarily connotes blessing as a form of comfort and support; how does the use of this word as the poem's title influence the reading of the poem?

6. The poet remarks in his interview that "True irony exists in nature. All we can do is try to reach it." What did you find to be one of the book's most memorable ironic moments?

SPECIAL TERMS

Agent Orange—a herbicide and defoliant sprayed by the U.S. military to clear large sections of vegetation and jungle to expose the enemy and make it difficult for the Viet Cong to hide or move around. It contaminated the water, soil, plants and trees throughout Vietnam and persisted long after the U.S. military left the country. It is linked to many cancers and other diseases, such as diabetes, and skin and gastrointestinal disorders suffered by the Vietnamese and U.S. soldiers who were exposed to it.

ARVN soldier—A South Vietnamese soldier.

AK-47—an automatic Russian assault rifle.

Angel's Wing—a section of Vietnam near the Cambodian Border, so called because of its shape on a military map.

APC—U.S. armored personnel carrier.

B-52—a U.S. bomber capable of dropping large, highly destructive bombs.

Berm—The dirt mound that surrounds a rice paddy; a dirt mound constructed around the perimeter of a fire base or base camp.

Bien Hoa—a large U.S. Air Force base near Saigon.

bomb water—brackish pools of water found in bomb craters; water in empty overhead 250-pound bomb shells equipped with a pipe, valve and pull chain for use by G.I.s in bathing.

Cau Dai—a Vietnamese religious sect whose patron saints are Buddha, Jesus and Victor Hugo. Their temple outside Tay Ninh is famous for its gold furnishings and a large sphere with the painting of an eye that symbolizes the Divine Eye overseeing the universe.

Chieu Hoi—translates to *open arms*. The U.S. Army instituted the Chieu Hoi program to induce Viet Cong to surrender. They were given amnesty in exchange for information or duty as scouts and informers. Many had been fighting in the jungle, living in tunnels and caves, since they were small children. Many of them were executed by the victorious North Vietnamese during the American withdrawal in 1975.

Chinook—a large transport helicopter with two sets of propellers used for transporting troops and supplies.

Claymore mine—a small antipersonnel mine hand detonated by a hand trigger device; sometimes placed inside an empty ammo can with nuts, bolts, nails and birdshot for maximum effect.

Cu Chi—main base camp of the U.S. 25th Infantry Division located not far from Saigon

Dominoes—a reference to the Domino Theory, one of the primary reasons espoused by John Foster Dulles, Secretary of State under President Eisenhower, and other Cold War ideologues for engaging in the Vietnam conflict. The theory held that if Vietnam fell to the socialist army of Ho Chi Minh the entire region would fall under Communist rule and Russian influence like a toppling series of standing dominoes lined up in a row.

Dau Tieng—a town in South Vietnam near the Michelin rubber plantation, a Viet Cong stronghold and the site of a large U.S. fire base. A unit dubbed "The Rubber Squad" was purportedly assigned the mission of counting and cataloguing the rubber trees in the plantation that were damaged or destroyed so that the U.S. government could reimburse the Michelin Rubber Company for its losses. The Rubber Squad "turned over" or had to be replaced often because of the high number of casualties they sustained. The mission of the Viet Cong hiding underground with a small space to allow room for the

116

barrels of their weapons was not to kill the members of the squad, but to shoot off the bottoms of their legs or otherwise cripple them so that Americans at home would see them hobbling about on crutches and theoretically intensify their protests of the war.

Gold—For many of the Vietnamese, gold—whether as teeth or fillings in their teeth, or in the jewelry that they wore or hid in makeshift cellars in the floors of their hooches—served as their savings accounts.

Hooch—a rural Vietnamese hut usually made of mud, bamboo or wooden posts and boards with a thatched or tin roof. The term was used by G.I.s for any small building or house where people lived.

LZ—landing zone.

McNamara—Robert McNamara, former president of Ford Motor Company and U.S. Secretary of State under Presidents Kennedy and Johnson. He resigned when Johnson refused to follow his advice to negotiate an end to the war which McNamara thought was a lost cause.

Mekong—a long, wide, muddy river that runs from headwaters in Tibet through South Vietnam into the South China sea. It was a busy route of commerce throughout the region and the scene of many battles with the Viet Cong. The area in the southern most section of South Vietnam was known as the Mekong Delta. The river and the delta were often simply referred to as the Mekong.

Napalm—a jellied gasoline mixture exploded on South Vietnamese military and civilian targets to cause horrifying burns and suffocation. Napalm sticks to the skin and flammable materials so that its effects are continuous and difficult to remove.

Nui Ba Din—The area in Tay Ninh Province was flat, in many ways resembling the American plains. Nui Ba Din was a lone mountain in the middle of the plain of very rough terrain where Buddhist monks were buried and Cambodian tigers were often spotted leaping from the flat ledges of the mountain side. The U.S. Army maintained a large radar facility at the top of the mountain, which was overrun on a regular basis. Duty at Nui Ba Din was considered highly hazardous. The Viet Cong often broadcast ghostly sounds and propaganda at night toward the camp. When seen at certain times of day, the mountain took on a dark cast for which it earned the name *Black Virgin Mountain*. Today the mountaintop is a theme park and the site of several Buddhist shrines that can be reached only by a ski lift.

RPG—rocket-propelled grenade.

Sapper—a Viet Cong or North Vietnamese commando. Sappers often slipped into U.S. or ARVN military fire bases or base camps with satchel charges made of plastic explosives.

Tay Ninh—a province of South Vietnam located in the northwestern corner of III Corp along the Cambodian Border. The U.S. Army maintained a large base near Tay Ninh City under the command of the 25th Infantry Division that looked out from one side onto Nui Ba Din.

Tet—an annual celebration of Buddha's birthday at the end of January coinciding with the start of the lunar new year. First Tet is the name given to Tet, 1968, in which the Viet Cong staged a large countrywide uprising that included an invasion of Saigon and dispelled the U.S. military's contention that the Viet Cong had been defeated. The following year the Viet Cong engaged in a smaller, less notorious attack known to G.I.s as Second Tet.

Ton Son Nhut—a South Vietnamese air base used regularly by the U.S. military. For many U.S. troops it was the first location in country where their feet hit the ground when they stepped off the transport plane from the United States.

Tunnel—Over the years beginning with their insurrections against the French colonialist regimes, the Viet Minh and Viet Cong painstakingly constructed intricate underground complexes that they used for a variety of purposes, including hideaways, ambushes, storage of weapons and ammunition, food, water and other supplies, field hospitals and resting places. During First Tet sappers emerged from tunnels into the heart of Cu Chi Base Camp. It is said that the Viet Cong dug the complexes one cupful at a time, handing cups or other small containers filled with dirt and rock down the line until it reached the Viet Cong at the entrance of the tunnel where their contents were dispersed under cover of darkness.

Tracer—a round of ammunition lit by phosphorous used to track the direction of a bullet. Outgoing tracers looked red; incoming tracers looked blue, at least from where the author of this book was located.

Victor Charlie—a male or female Viet Cong soldier or combatant.

Wire—the perimeter or berm of a fire base or base camp constructed with barbed wire or rolls of barbed wire.

COLOPHON

Cover and book design: Linda D. Brennaman
Editorial Assistant: Linda D. Brennaman
Assistant Managing Editor: Susan L. Schurman
Managing Editor: Ben Furnish
Executive Editor: Robert Stewart
BkMk Press wishes to thank Bradley Hoffman,
Marie Mayhugh, Zakiya Williams
Printer: Bookmobile, Minneapolis, Minnesota

First edition cover design by Deanna Bushéy
First edition Typesetting and book design by Action Type

This edition is printed on acid-free paper with the interior
type set in Arrus BT. The cover fonts used are Minion Pro,
Arial, and Optima.